ALPHONSE MUCHA'S
ART NOUVEAU
-A VINTAGE COLORING BOOK-
VOLUME 1

Inside these pages, you'll find over
30 beautiful monchrome prints
by Art Nouveau master, Alphonse Mucha.
The pictures were hand selected
and edited for maximum coloring enjoyment.

There's no right or wrong to way to color,
so grab your pencils
and take a trip through time.
Each coloring page is one sided
for easy removal and display.

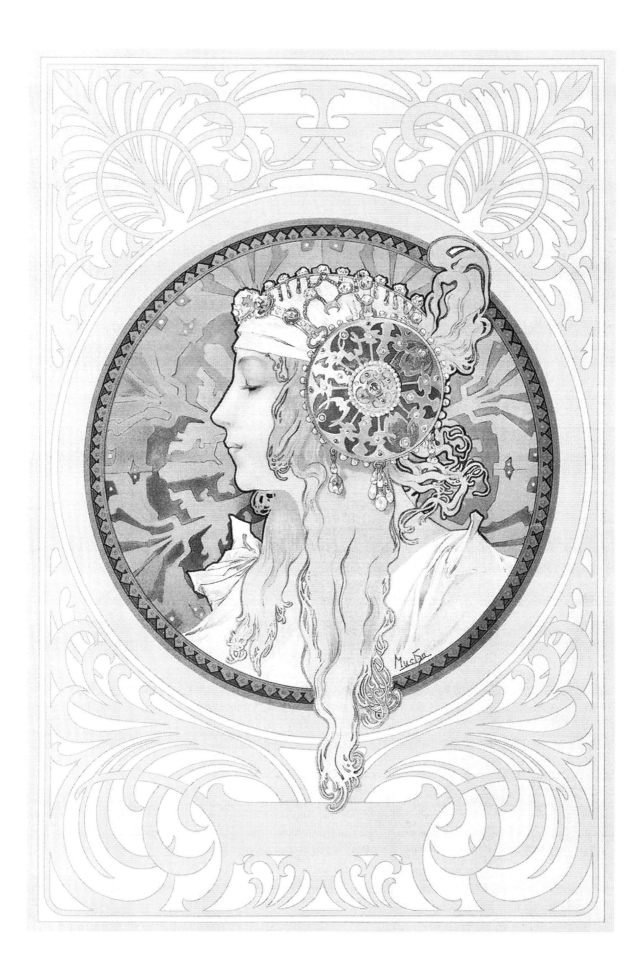

AU QUARTIER LATIN

Prix: 0,60

Numéro exceptionnel
NOEL 1900
DIRECTEUR: P. CARLO-BUNODE.

EXPOSITION UNIVERSELLE & INTERNATIONALE
DE St LOUIS (ÉTATS-UNIS)
DU 30 AVRIL AU 30 NOVEMBRE 1904.

DE PARIS A St LOUIS
6 JOURS DE STEAMER
ET 1 JOUR DE CHEMIN DE FER

IMPORTANCE DE L'EXPOSITION

PHILADELPHIE	1876	95 HECTARES		CHICAGO	1893	240 HECTARES
PARIS	1900	135 HECTARES		St LOUIS	1904	500 HECTARES

IMP. F. CHAMPENOIS _ PARIS

CLAIR de LUNE

ÉTOILE POLAIRE

ÉTOILE du SOIR

ÉTOILE du MATIN

CHANSONS D'AÏEULES

DITES par Mucha
MADAME AMEL
de la Comédie Française.

-THE END-

43026276R00046

Made in the USA
Lexington, KY
15 July 2015